Note to Librarians, Teachers, and Parents:

Blastoff! Readers are carefully developed by literacy experts and combine standards-based content with developmentally appropriate text.

Level 1 provides the most support through repetition of high-frequency words, light text, predictable sentence patterns, and strong visual support.

Level 2 offers early readers a bit more challenge through varied simple sentences, increased text load, and less repetition of high-frequency words.

Level 3 advances early-fluent readers toward fluency through increased text and concept load, less reliance on visuals, longer sentences, and more literary language.

Level 4 builds reading stamina by providing more text per page, increased use of punctuation, greater variation in sentence patterns, and increasingly challenging vocabulary.

Level 5 encourages children to move from "learning to read" to "reading to learn" by providing even more text, varied writing styles, and less familiar topics.

Whichever book is right for your reader, Blastoff! Readers are the perfect books to build confidence and encourage a love of reading that will last a lifetime!

This edition first published in 2018 by Bellwether Media, Inc.

No part of this publication may be reproduced in whole or in part without written permission of the publisher. For information regarding permission, write to Bellwether Media, Inc., Attention: Permissions Department, 5357 Penn Avenue South, Minneapolis, MN 55419.

Library of Congress Cataloging-in-Publication Data

Names: Sommer, Nathan, author.
Title: Angelfish / by Nathan Sommer.
Description: Minneapolis, MN : Bellwether Media, Inc., [2018] | Series: Blastoff! Readers. Ocean Life Up Close | Audience: Age 5-8. | Audience: K to Grade 3. | Includes bibliographical references and index.
Identifiers: LCCN 2017028810| ISBN 9781626177642 (hardcover : alk. paper) | ISBN 9781681034737 (ebook)
Subjects: LCSH: Marine angelfishes–Juvenile literature.
Classification: LCC QL638.P768 S66 2018 | DDC 597/.72–dc23
LC record available at https://lccn.loc.gov/2017028810

Text copyright © 2018 by Bellwether Media, Inc. BLASTOFF! READERS and associated logos are trademarks and/or registered trademarks of Bellwether Media, Inc. SCHOLASTIC, CHILDREN'S PRESS, and associated logos are trademarks and/or registered trademarks of Scholastic Inc., 557 Broadway, New York, NY 10012.

Editor: Paige V. Polinsky   Designer: Brittany McIntosh

Printed in the United States of America, North Mankato, MN.

Table of Contents

What Are Angelfish?	4
Flat and Flashy	8
Reef Eaters	14
Baby Angels	20
Glossary	22
To Learn More	23
Index	24

What Are Angelfish?

royal angelfish

Angelfish are known for their rich colors. More than 80 different types of these fish swim in the world's oceans.

Their bright bodies blend in with their surroundings.

French angelfish

Angelfish like warm, **tropical** waters. They live in the Atlantic, Pacific, and Indian oceans.

yellowband angelfish

Species Spotlight
QUEEN ANGELFISH

life span:
up to 15 years

depth range:
0 to 230 feet
(0 to 70 meters)

queen angelfish range = ▢

conservation status: least concern

| Extinct | Extinct in the Wild | Critically Endangered | Endangered | Vulnerable | Near Threatened | Least Concern |

These fish often make their homes in **coral reefs**.

Flat and Flashy

Angelfish come in every color of the rainbow. Some are shiny silver. Many have stripes, spots, or freckles.

crown

Some angelfish have yellow markings around their eyes. Others have blue spots called crowns on their heads.

Angelfish have flat, thin bodies. This allows them to easily hide in cracks and between **corals**.

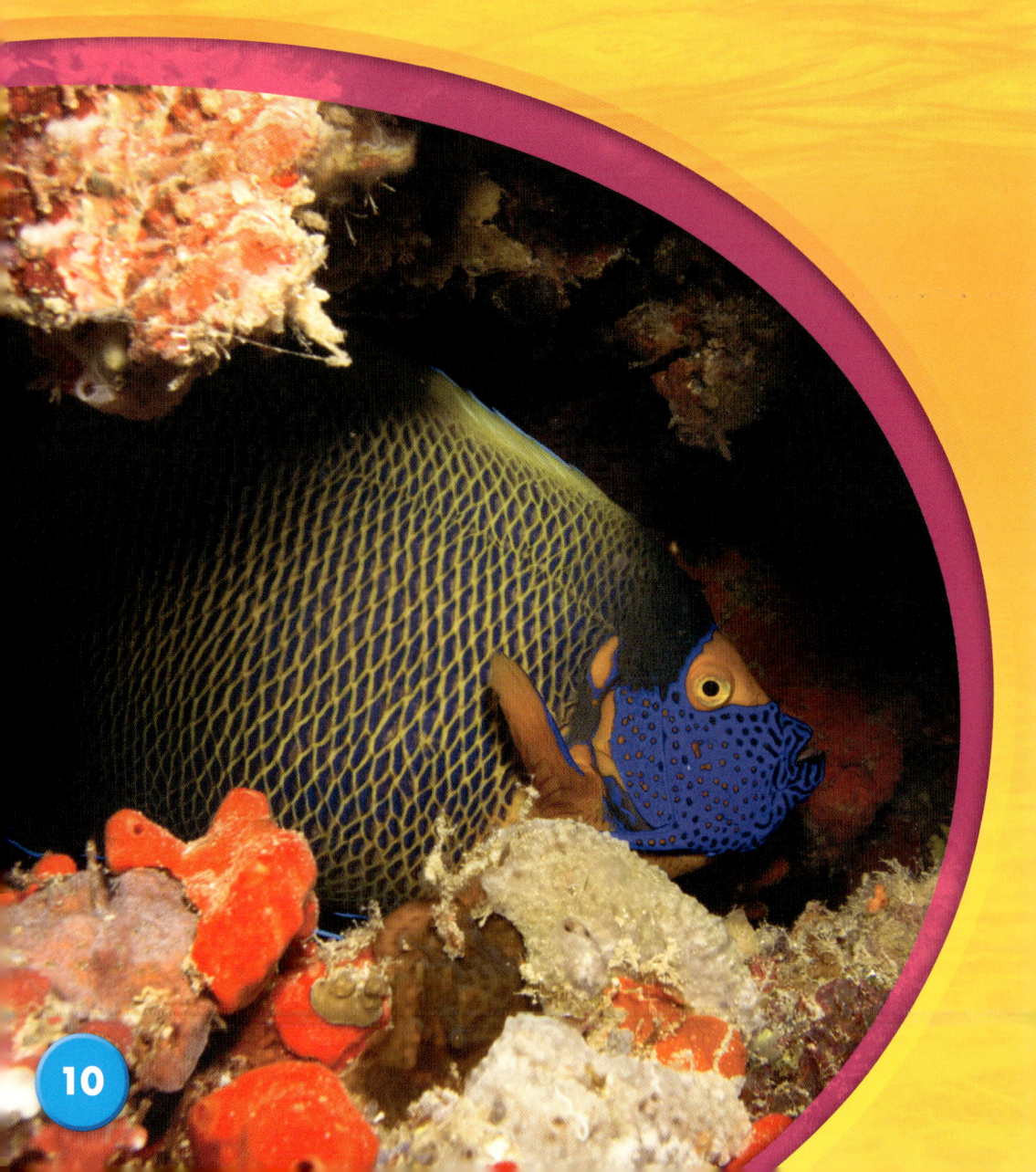

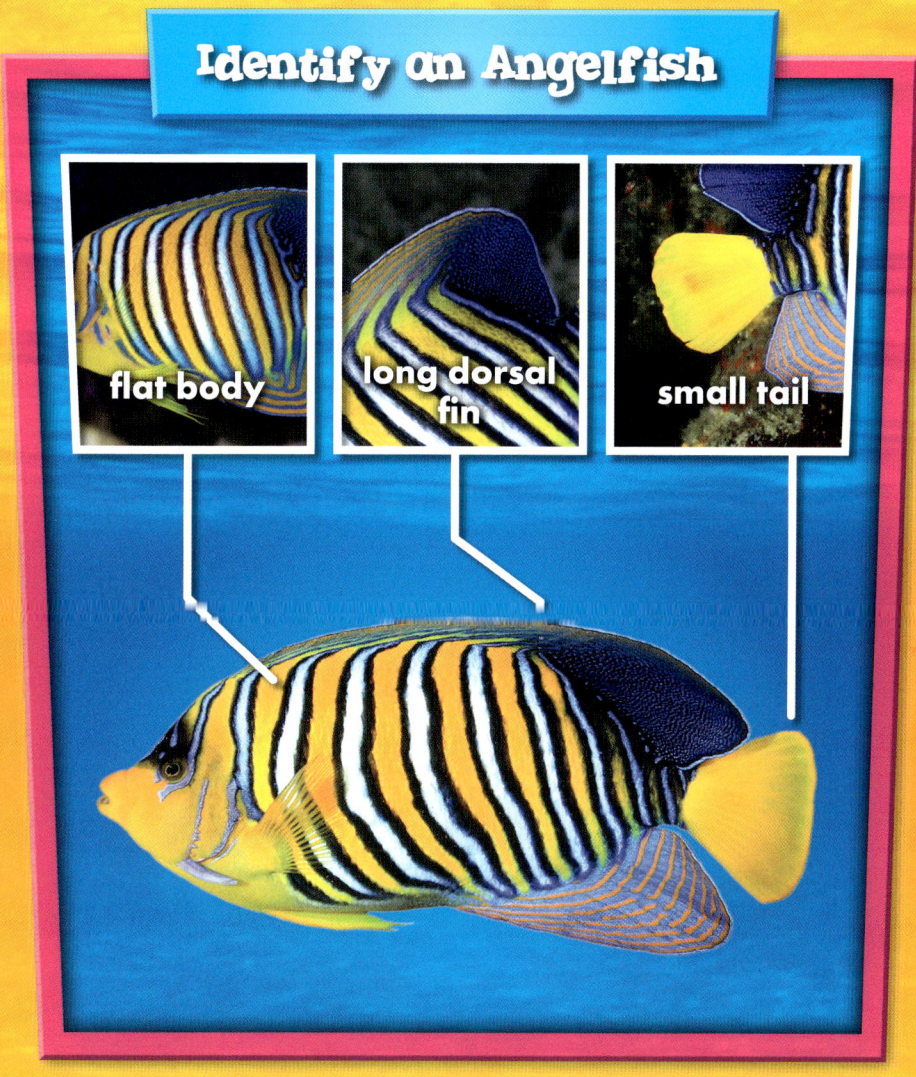

Long **dorsal fins** give angelfish a triangle-shaped look. Their tails are small and bright.

Angelfish have small, pointed mouths. They also have sharp **spines** by their cheeks.

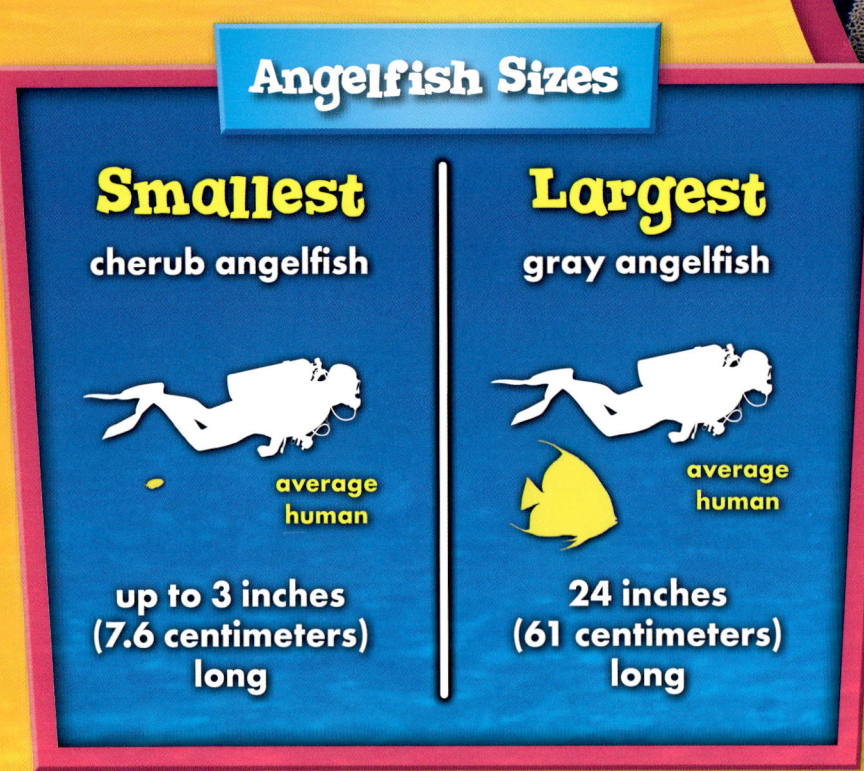

Angelfish Sizes

Smallest	Largest
cherub angelfish	gray angelfish
average human	average human
up to 3 inches (7.6 centimeters) long	24 inches (61 centimeters) long

gray angelfish

spine

cherub angelfish

Some angelfish are less than 3 inches (7.6 centimeters) long. Others can grow as big as 24 inches (61 centimeters) long!

Reef Eaters

Angelfish use rows of strong teeth to eat hard sponges and corals. But these **omnivores** are not picky. They also like to eat **algae** and small **invertebrates**.

The fish usually feed during the day and hide at night.

Catch of the Day

tube sponges

green algae

elkhorn corals

blue ring angelfish

15

Angelfish are slow but skilled swimmers. Their thin bodies allow them to slip through plants to avoid being eaten.

Without hiding spots, angelfish can be easy for **predators** to spot.

bicolor angelfish

Angelfish mostly live alone or in small **schools**. But they may spend time with others. They help other fish by cleaning them.

These angelfish wait in busy spots along the reef. They eat **parasites** off the fish that swim up to them.

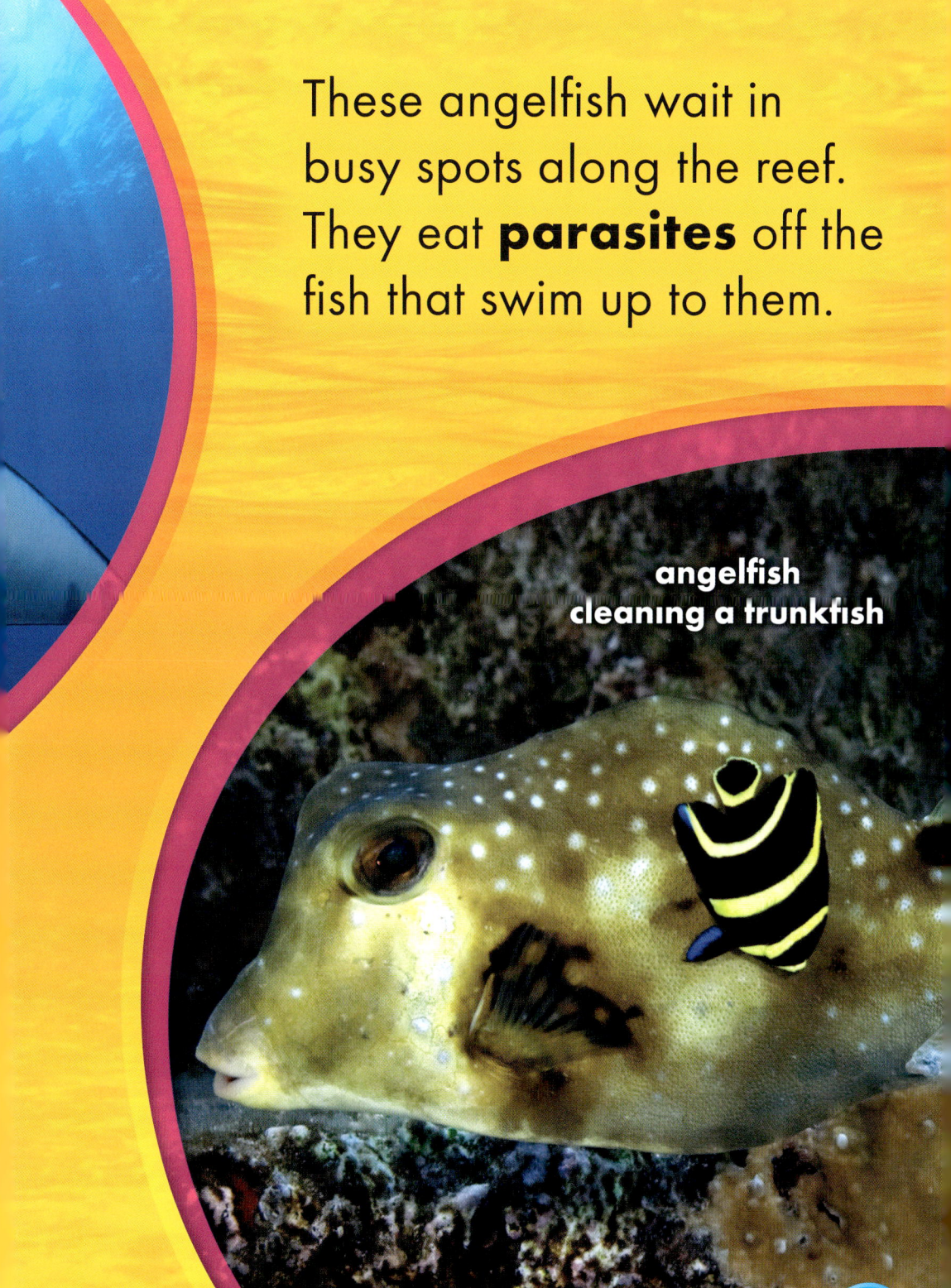

angelfish cleaning a trunkfish

Baby Angels

baby lemonpeel angelfish

Baby angelfish begin life as eggs floating in the water. After about a day, they turn into tiny **larvae**.

The larvae grow fast. They will soon change colors as they become adults!

adult emperor angelfish with baby

Glossary

algae—plants and plantlike living things; most kinds of algae grow in water.

coral reefs—structures made of coral that usually grow in shallow seawater

corals—the living ocean animals that build coral reefs

dorsal fins—the fins on top of angelfish backs

invertebrates—animals without backbones

larvae—early, tiny forms of an animal that must go through a big change to become adults

omnivores—animals that eat both plants and animals

parasites—living things that survive on or in other living things; parasites offer nothing for the food and protection they receive.

predators—animals that hunt other animals for food

schools—groups of fish

spines—sharp, pointed body parts

tropical—related to the tropics; the tropics is a hot region near the equator.

To Learn More

AT THE LIBRARY

Rattini, Kristin. *National Geographic Readers: Coral Reefs.* Washington, D.C.: National Geographic, 2015.

Schuetz, Kari. *Life in a Coral Reef.* Minneapolis, Minn.: Bellwether Media, 2016.

Schuh, Mari. *Parrotfish.* Minneapolis, Minn.: Bellwether Media, 2017.

ON THE WEB

Learning more about angelfish is as easy as 1, 2, 3.

1. Go to www.factsurfer.com.

2. Enter "angelfish" into the search box.

3. Click the "Surf" button and you will see a list of related web sites.

With factsurfer.com, finding more information is just a click away.

Index

babies, 20
bodies, 5, 10, 11, 17
cleaning, 18, 19
colors, 4, 8, 9, 21
coral reefs, 7, 19
crowns, 9
depth, 7
dorsal fins, 11
eggs, 20
food, 14, 15, 19
heads, 9
hide, 10, 14, 17
larvae, 20, 21
life span, 7
markings, 8, 9
mouths, 12
omnivores, 14
parasites, 19
predators, 16, 17
range, 6, 7
schools, 18
sizes, 12, 13
spines, 12, 13
status, 7

swim, 4, 17, 19
tails, 11
teeth, 14
types, 4

The images in this book are reproduced through the courtesy of: PAUL ATKINSON, front cover, pp. 11 (top right), 13 (bottom); Rich Carey, pp. 3, 4, 11 (top left, bottom), 16 (bottom); Marli Wakeling/ Alamy, p. 5; 3/ NaturePL/ SuperStock, p. 6; Christian Delbert, p. 7; Image Source/ SuperStock, p. 8; Global_Pics, p. 9; amooo, p. 10; DJ Mattaar, p. 11 (top center); Michael Rothschild, p. 13 (top); Laura Dinraths, p. 15 (top left); Jcwait/ Wikipedia, p. 15 (top center); John A. Anderson, p. 15 (top right); imageBROKER/ Alamy, p. 15 (bottom); kaschibo, p. 16 (top left); Matt9122, p. 16 (top center); Yann hubert, p. 16 (top right); Andrii Slonchak, p. 17; Claudio Contreras/ Nature Picture Library, p. 18; Universal Images Group/ SuperStock, p. 19; zaferkizilkaya, p. 20; F.Bettex - lookandprint.com/ Alamy, p. 21.